AMAZING HOCKEY TRIVIA FOR KIDS

Eric Zweig

illustrations by
Jeff Martin

Scholastic Canada Ltd.
Toronto New York London Auckland Sydney
Mexico City New Delhi Hong Kong Buenos Aires

For Amanda, once again.
— Eric

Scholastic Canada Ltd.
604 King Street West, Toronto, Ontario M5V 1E1, Canada

Scholastic Inc.
557 Broadway, New York, NY 10012, USA

Scholastic Australia Pty Limited
PO Box 579, Gosford, NSW 2250, Australia

Scholastic New Zealand Limited
Private Bag 94407, Botany, Manukau 2163, New Zealand

Scholastic Children's Books
1 London Bridge, London SE1 9BG, UK

www.scholastic.ca

Library and Archives Canada Cataloguing in Publication
Title: Amazing hockey trivia for kids / Eric Zweig ; illustrations by Jeff Martin.
Names: Zweig, Eric, 1963- author. | Martin, Jeff, 1986- illustrator.
Description: Series statement: Hockey trivia for kids ; 6
Identifiers: Canadiana 20240328760 | ISBN 9781039707627 (softcover)
Subjects: LCSH: National Hockey League—Miscellanea—Juvenile literature. | LCSH: Hockey—Miscellanea— Juvenile literature. | LCGFT: Trivia and miscellanea.
Classification: LCC GV847.25 .Z937 2024 | DDC j796.962—dc23

CREDITS
Photos ©: cover, i: Andy Devlin/NHLI via Getty Images; 11: Meng Yongmin/Xinhua via Getty Images; 47: Women with Plexiglas shields, Maple Leaf Gardens, City of Toronto Archives, Fonds 1257, Series 1057, Item 7478; 60: Andrew Lahodynskyj/NHLI via Getty Images; 91: Glenn James/NHLI via Getty Images; 93: Dave Sandford/NHLI via Getty Images; 111: Canada Post © 2020.

Text copyright © 2024 by Eric Zweig.
Illustrations copyright © 2024 by Scholastic Canada Ltd.
All rights reserved.

No part of this publication may be reproduced or stored in a retrieval system, or transmitted in any form or by any means, electronic, mechanical, recording, or otherwise, without written permission of the publisher, Scholastic Canada Ltd., 604 King Street West, Toronto, Ontario M5V 1E1, Canada. In the case of photocopying or other reprographic copying, a licence must be obtained from Access Copyright (Canadian Copyright Licensing Agency), www.accesscopyright.ca or 1-800-893-5777.

6 5 4 3 2 1   Printed in Canada 114   24 25 26 27 28

MIX
Paper | Supporting responsible forestry
FSC® C016245
www.fsc.org

Introduction

It's hard to believe that my first *Hockey Trivia for Kids* book came out in 2006! Back then I didn't realize it would be the first in a series, and I included all the great old hockey stories I knew. Fortunately, there are lots of great stories — enough to fill a lot of books. I still love the history of hockey, but my most recent books have lots of current hockey stories too. And a lot of what's new still echoes back to my old favourites. So I hope you'll find some familiar things and that you'll also learn something new about the history of hockey. Mostly I hope you'll have fun reading it!

Halifax Home Games

Like a lot of players, Sidney Crosby left home at a young age to pursue a career in hockey. The native of Cole Harbour, Nova Scotia, last played for a Halifax area team — the Dartmouth Subways under-18 team — in 2001–02, when he was 14 years old. His last game in Halifax before he went pro came at the end of his second and final season of junior hockey. On May 10, 2005, his team, Rimouski Oceanic, defeated the Halifax Mooseheads 4–3 to sweep the championship final of the Quebec Major Junior Hockey League. When Crosby was named the playoff MVP, the crowd cheered for him, even though he helped beat the local team. "It's an amazing feeling to do this at home — it doesn't get much better," Crosby said. He was 17 years old.

After his stellar rookie season in the NHL with Pittsburgh in 2005–06, Crosby made his first visit to Halifax as a professional player when his Penguins played the Ottawa Senators in an exhibition game on September 19, 2006. Crosby had a goal and an assist, but Ottawa won the game 5–2. Still only 19 years old at the time, he was truly "Sid the Kid."

It would be 17 years before another NHL pre-season exhibition game in Crosby's hometown. Again, his Penguins took on the Senators in the Nova Scotia Showdown at the Scotiabank Centre in Halifax on October 2, 2023. By then he was 36 years old. A crowd of 11,093 packed the arena and gave Crosby a long standing ovation before the game started. Once again, Ottawa won the game, this time 3–0. Obviously, Crosby got no points, but he was still chosen as the game's third star.

DiD YOU KNOW?

In 2018, the Nova Scotia Sports Hall of Fame unveiled a list of the top 15 sports stars from the province. Sidney Crosby was chosen as the best athlete ever from Nova Scotia.

Amazing Race

Before the Monday, October 2, 2023, exhibition game, Crosby led his teammates in bonding activities all weekend, including an *Amazing Race*–style contest. Some of the events included shucking oysters, eating haggis, running up the hill at the Halifax Citadel (part of Crosby's off-season training regimen), learning to tie a bowline knot at the Maritime Museum and carrying kegs at a brewery. Evgeni Malkin claimed victory for his team in the contest.

BFFs

With the opening of the 2023–24 NHL season on October 10, 2023, Sidney Crosby, Evgeni Malkin and Kris Letang became the longest-tenured trio of teammates in the history of North American professional sports. The three played together for their 18th season, surpassing the 17 seasons Derek Jeter, Jorge Posada and Mariano Rivera all played with baseball's New York Yankees from 1995 through 2011. The three Penguins teammates began playing together in 2006–07, when Malkin and Letang were rookies and Crosby was beginning his second NHL season.

NAME GAME
Team Names

The Halifax Mooseheads were the first Canadian franchise in the Quebec Major Junior Hockey League (QMJHL) based outside of Quebec. They began play in the Nova Scotia capital in the 1994–95 season. The team was named after a local brewery.

QMJHL, M, N, O, P

The top junior league in the province of Quebec was originally founded in 1969. For years it was known as the Quebec Major Junior Hockey League ... or the QMJHL for short. These days the league has 12 Quebec-based teams and 6 other teams in New Brunswick, Nova Scotia and Prince Edward Island. In December of 2023, the "M" in the name was changed from "Major" to "Maritimes."

All-New Original Six

After years of trying to organize a new league that would bring together the top women hockey players in the world, it was announced on August 29, 2023, that the Professional Women's Hockey League (PWHL) would begin play in 2023–24. There were six teams in the PWHL that first season. Three are based in Canada: in Montreal, Toronto and Ottawa. The three others are in the United States: in Boston, New York and Minnesota. Future expansion is planned.

DiD YOU KNOW?

The original Original Six aren't the teams that were in the NHL when it first formed in 1917. Instead, they were the only six teams in the league from 1942–1967: the Toronto Maple Leafs, the Montreal Canadiens, the Detroit Red Wings, the New York Rangers, the Chicago Black Hawks and the Boston Bruins.

Happy New League!

On January 1, 2024, the PWHL began its first season when New York visited Toronto at a sold-out Mattamy Athletic Centre in downtown Toronto. (Toronto sold out all its home games before the season even started!) Unfortunately for the hometown crowd, New York won the game 4–0. Ella Shelton scored the first-ever PWHL goal on a shot from the point after a face-off won by teammate Alex Carpenter at 10:43 of the first period. Other historic PWHL firsts from that game include:

FIRST	PLAYER	TEAM
Faceoff win	Alex Carpenter	New York
Shot	Ella Shelton	New York
Save	Kristen Campbell	Toronto
Penalty (slashing)	Rebecca Leslie	Toronto
Shutout	Corinne Schroeder	New York

PWHL Play List

The draft to stock the new PWHL teams was held on September 18, 2023, announced by tennis legend Billie Jean King. Each of the six teams was able to select 15 players. The first pick was Taylor Heise of Lake City, Minnesota, who starred at the University of Minnesota for five seasons. Unsurprisingly, she was chosen by the Minnesota team.

Of the 90 players chosen in the first PWHL Draft, most were from Canada (48) or the United States (29). There were also 13 players chosen from seven European countries: Austria (1), Czechia (5), Finland (2), France (1), Germany (1), Sweden (2) and Switzerland (1).

Before the first draft was held, each team was allowed to sign three players as free agents. All nine players who signed with the Canadian-based teams have been members of the Canadian women's national team. Eight of the nine who signed with American teams have been members of the U.S. national team. Here's a look at those signings:

TEAM, PLAYER	POSITION	HOMETOWN
MONTREAL		
Marie-Philip Poulin	Forward	Beauceville, Quebec
Laura Stacey	Forward	Mississauga, Ontario
Ann-Renée Desbiens	Goaltender	La Malbaie, Quebec
TORONTO		
Sarah Nurse	Forward	Hamilton, Ontario
Renata Fast	Defence	Hamiton, Ontario
Blayre Turnbull	Forward	Stellarton, Nova Scotia
OTTAWA		
Brianne Jenner	Forward	Oakville, Ontario
Emerance Maschmeyer	Goaltender	Bruderheim, Alberta
Emily Clark	Forward	Saskatoon, Saskatchewan
BOSTON		
Hilary Knight	Forward	Palo Alto, California
Megan Keller	Defence	Farmington, Michigan
Aerin Frankel	Goaltender	New York, New York
MINNESOTA		
Kendall Coyne Schofield	Forward	Palos Heights, Illinois
Kelly Pannek	Forward	Plymouth, Minnesota
Lee Secklein	Defence	Roseville, Minnesota
NEW YORK		
Abby Roque	Forward	Potsdam, New York
Micah Zandee-Harrt	Defence	Saanichton, British Columbia
Alex Carpenter	Forward	North Reading, Massachusetts

MASCOT MAYHEM

Blades the Bruin is the mascot for the Boston Bruins. Blades has been the Bruins mascot since 1999. (He isn't a real bear; he's a person in a bear costume.) Blades was named by nine-year-old Jillian Dempsey, who grew up to be more than just a lifelong Bruins fan. She became a hockey star herself, playing with the Boston Blades of the Canadian Women's Hockey League and the Boston Pride in the Premier Hockey Federation (formerly the National Women's Hockey League) from 2013 to 2023, when it ceased operations. Dempsey was captain of the Boston Pride for six seasons and the PHF's all-time leader in games played (142), goals (70), assists (76) and points (146).

Dempsey was selected by Montreal — not Boston! — in the Professional Women's Hockey League first draft.

Record Setter

Sarah Nurse set a new Olympic hockey record for most points at the the 2022 Winter Olympics in Beijing. She earned 18, topping the previous record of 17, set by Hayley Wickenheiser in 2006. Nurse scored 5 goals and had 13 assists, leading Canada to a gold medal. Nurse had previously won gold at the World Championships in 2021, but the victory in Beijing made her the first Black player to win Olympic gold in women's hockey. Twenty years earlier, Jarome Iginla was the first Black man to win a gold medal in men's hockey after Canada's 5-2 victory over the United States at the 2002 Salt Lake City Games.

Sarah Nurse battles for the puck in the gold medal game on Feb. 17, 2022.

Ice Queen

Before she was queen, Princess Elizabeth and her husband, Prince Philip, visited Canada for the first time in the fall of 1951. On October 13, they attended a 15-minute exhibition hockey game between the Leafs and Black Hawks. It was a fundraiser for children with disabilities, with around 14,000 fans in attendance. They next attended an NHL game in Montreal on October 29, when the Canadiens defeated the New York Rangers 6–1. The royal couple found the games very entertaining, with Prince Philip especially enjoying the hard hits.

Elizabeth became Queen in 1952 and it would be 50 years before she went to another hockey game. On October 6, 2002, she dropped the puck for the ceremonial opening faceoff at a preseason game in Vancouver between the Canucks and the San Jose Sharks. When she arrived for the event, the Queen walked a red carpet along with Wayne Gretzky, Olympic hockey gold medalists Ed Jovanovski and Cassie Campbell... and legendary hockey broadcaster Howie Meeker.

Eighty-eight-year-old Meeker had played for the Maple Leafs back in that royal exhibition back in 1951. According to Meeker, it was the queen herself who wanted to invite someone who'd played in that game 51 years before. He even got to talk to the queen about the old game. Meeker was thrilled. "It was a great day for hockey," he said. "It was a great day for Canada. It was a great day for the queen, I think. She really enjoyed it near as I can tell."

The Golden . . . Puck?

Maurice "Rocket" Richard scored twice for the Canadiens when Princess Elizabeth and Prince Philip saw him play in Montreal in 1951. The Prince chatted with the Rocket at the game that night. The next year, on November 8, Richard broke the NHL scoring record with his 325th career goal. The Canadiens had the puck plated in gold and sent as a gift to the new queen.

Did You Know?

On February 14, 1895, a hockey game was played on the grounds of Buckingham Palace. Members of the royal staff, including the future King Edward VII (on defence) and his son, the future King George V (a forward), faced off against a team of British Parliament members. The Princes' team won in an 8–5 victory. One of the players on the opposing team was Lord Edward Stanley, the son of Lord Frederick Arthur Stanley, who donated the Stanley Cup to Canadian hockey in 1893.

Stuck Puck

Pucks are small, and sometimes they're hard to see. Every now and then a goalie will make a save and the puck disappears into their equipment. It can get caught between a pad and the goalie's leg, or even trapped in their pants. But in a game on December 5, 2023, the puck pulled a new trick. Playing against the Nashville Predators, Chicago defenceman Connor Murphy attempted to chip the puck out of the Blackhawks' zone. The puck flew up, sailed over the top of the glass, struck a camera, and then landed — perfectly balanced — sitting atop the glass.

Double Take

There have been a few different NHL players who have the same name. Vancouver has two players named Elias Petterson in their organization. Two NHL goalies are named Matt Murray, and there used to be a Niklas Backstrom and a Nicklas Backstrom. Still, a playoff game between the Carolina Hurricanes and the New York Islanders on April 25, 2023, may have been the only time that two players with the same name sat in the penalty box at the same time. Sebastian Aho of the Islanders was in the penalty box for holding at 11:51 of the third period. A little more than a minute later, Sebastian Aho of the Hurricanes was sent off at 13:09 for high-sticking.

Name Game
Classic Edition

Though his teammates from his junior days nicknamed him "Axe," fans called Gary Smith "Suitcase." That's because Smith played for a lot of teams in his career — 6 NHL teams with 7 different names in 14 seasons between 1965 and 1978. Smith tended goal for the Toronto Maple Leafs, the Oakland Seals/California Golden Seals, the Chicago Black Hawks, the Vancouver Canucks, the Minnesota North Stars and the Winnipeg Jets. "Suitcase" also played for the Jets and the Indianapolis Racers in the World Hockey Association.

Have Pads, Will Travel

Gary Smith had nothing on a goalie named Marv Edwards. Edwards was 34 years old before he even played his first NHL game with the Pittsburgh Penguins on February 20, 1969. Before that, Edwards had spent 19 years, dating back to 1950, playing as an amateur and as a pro with teams in 17 different cities! During the 1954–55 season, Edwards set a unique hockey record that may never be broken.

On the afternoon of December 19, 1954, Edwards was with his St. Catharines junior team playing against St. Michael's College in Toronto. St. Mikes' won 4–1, but during the game, St. Catharines coach Rudy Pilous found out that his goalie would be needed that night in Buffalo to join the Bisons of the American Hockey League.

So after the game in Toronto, Pilous loaded Edwards into a car with his goalie gear and a couple of sandwiches, and he took off for Buffalo. They were making good time ... until the car ran out of gas!

Determined to make it to the game, Edwards grabbed his hockey bag and hitchhiked his way across the border to Buffalo. He arrived just in time for the game. Edwards played well, but the Bisons were beaten 3–2 by the Pittsburgh Hornets in overtime. Still, despite his two losses, Edwards had set a record by playing with two different teams, in two different leagues, in two different cities, in two different countries, all in one day.

Golden Misfits

Most expansion teams take years to become successful, but the Vegas Golden Knights stunned everyone by reaching the Stanley Cup Final in their very first season, 2017–18. Like most expansion teams, the Golden Knights were built mainly of players cast off by other teams. The players rallied around their outsider status, calling themselves "The Golden Misfits." Six of the original Golden Misfits were still on the team when Vegas won the Stanley Cup in 2023. They were William Carrier, William Karlsson, Jonathan Marchessault, Brayden McNabb, Reilly Smith and Shea Theodore.

When the Golden Knights won the final, captain Mark Stone knew that after he got to skate around with the Cup first, he wanted the next player to receive it to be one of the Misfits. He passed it to Smith, who gave it to Marchesssault, who gave it to Karlsson. Those three players had played in every Vegas playoff game since the team's first season.

Hats Off

Golden Knights captain Mark Stone scored three goals when Vegas beat the Florida Panthers 9–3 in the fifth and deciding game of the 2023 Stanley Cup Final. It marked the first time in 101 years that a player had scored a hat trick in a Cup-clinching game. The last player to do so was Babe Dye of the Toronto St. Pats, who actually scored four goals in a 5–1 win over the Vancouver Millionaires on March 28, 1922.

BY THE NUMBERS

With their 9-3 victory over Florida to win the 2023 Stanley Cup, Vegas scored the most goals in a Cup-clinching game in NHL history. The only teams to score nine goals or more in a game when they won the Stanley Cup all did so before the NHL's first season of 1917-18. Here's a look at the list:

SCORE	WINNING TEAM	LOSING TEAM	YEAR
23-2	Ottawa Silver Seven	Dawson City Klondikers	1905
15-2	Montreal Victorias	Ottawa Capitals	1897
13-1	Montreal Wanderers	Ottawa Victorias	1908
13-7	Ottawa Senators	Edmonton Hockey Club	1910
13-4	Ottawa Senators	Port Arthur Hockey Club	1911
12-7	Ottawa Silver Seven	Queen's University	1906
12-3	Vancouver Millionaires	Ottawa Senators	1915
11-2	Ottawa Silver Seven	Toronto Marlboros	1904
9-3	Ottawa Silver Seven	Brandon Hockey Club	1904
9-3	Montreal Wanderers	Winnipeg Maple Leafs	1908
9-1	Seattle Metropolitans	Montreal Canadiens	1917

Trophy Tales

It's been a yearly tradition since 1924 for the players on the winning team to have their names engraved on the Stanley Cup. In 1993 players on the winning team were first given their own official day to spend with it in the summer after they won it. In 1995 the NHL made it an annual event. But it wasn't until the summer of 2023 that the winning players got to see their names on the Stanley Cup on their special day with the trophy.

Traditionally, names were engraved onto the Stanley Cup at the end of the summer. That is until Bill Foley, owner of the Vegas Golden Knights, suggested a change. His team had just won the 2023 Stanley Cup. Foley knew how special it would be for the team members to see their names on the Cup when they had their turn with it and were celebrating with family and friends. Foley asked the NHL to engrave the names immediately after the NHL Awards ceremony (which takes place a week or two after the Stanley Cup Final) instead of waiting until September, after everyone had already had their day with the Cup. Now, players can show off their names on the trophy while they celebrate with it on their big day.

Kings and Coyotes and Kangaroos

On September 23 and 24, 2023, the Los Angeles Kings and the Arizona Coyotes played a pair of exhibition games in Melbourne, Australia. They were the first NHL games ever played in the southern hemisphere. The games were played at the Rod Laver Arena, where the Australian Open tennis tournament is held each January.

The two hockey games were sellouts at the 13,000-seat arena, with a crowd of 13,097 at the Saturday game and 13,118 on Sunday. Arizona won the first game 5–3, with Clayton Keller of the Coyotes scoring the first NHL goal in Australia. Adrian Kempe, who scored once for Los Angeles in that game, scored twice for the Kings in the second contest to lead them to a 3–2 victory.

DID YOU KNOW?

When the Arizona Coyotes traded Nick Ritchie and Tony Stecher to the Calgary Flames on March 3, 2023, for Brett Ritchie and Connor Mackey, it marked the first brother-for-brother trade in NHL history.

High-Scoring Siblings

Paul Kariya was a slick playmaker and stylish star with the Anaheim Ducks, Colorado Avalanche, Nashville Predators and St. Louis Blues for 15 seasons in the NHL from 1994 to 2010. Though he never led the league in scoring, Kariya ranked among the top 10 four times and had more than 100 points in a season twice. A series of serious injuries slowed him down during his career, but he was still elected to the Hockey Hall of Fame in 2017.

Paul's younger brother, Steve Kariya, played 65 games during parts of three seasons in the NHL from 1999 to 2002. Youngest brother Martin Kariya never made the NHL, but both he and Steve played several years in Europe. In fact, Steve and Martin Kariya are the only brothers to have both won the Veli-Pekka Ketola Trophy as the leading scorer in the Finnish Elite League.

Oh Brothers!

Brothers Pierre-Olivier Joseph of the Pittsburgh Penguins and Mathieu Joseph of the Ottawa Senators received simultaneous penalties for high-sticking each other on the same play in a game on January 20, 2023. The bottom part of Pierre-Olivier's stick hit Mathieu in the face when Pierre-Olivier was trying to check his big brother. Then Pierre-Olivier managed to hit himself in the face with the other end of his own stick. Even so, the referee gave penalties to both brothers while the TV cameras showed their parents sitting in the stands shaking their heads in disbelief. It was the first time that the two had faced each other in an NHL game. Little brother Pierre-Olivier's team won, 4–1.

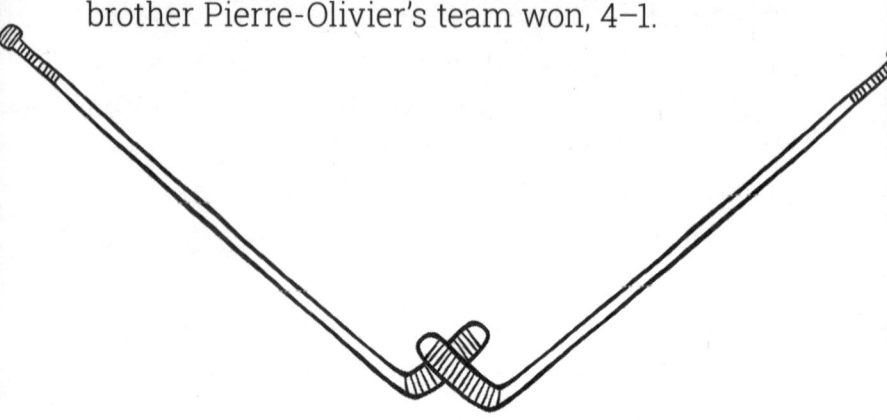

Pass the Cup

A record seven different members of the Patrick family have won the Stanley Cup. Lester Patrick won as a player with the Montreal Wanderers in 1906 and 1907, as coach, general manager and team owner with the Victoria Cougars in 1925 and as a coach and/or GM with the New York Rangers in 1928, 1933 and 1940.

Lester's sons, Lynn Patrick and Muzz Patrick, were players on the Rangers when they won the Cup in 1940. Lester's brother, Frank Patrick, was a player-coach-GM-owner of the Vancouver Millionaires when they won the Stanley Cup in 1915.

Lynn Patrick's son, Craig Patrick, played for eight seasons in the NHL. However, he is best remembered as the general manager of the Pittsburgh Penguins for many years, including 1991 and 1992 when the Penguins won the Stanley Cup.

Muzz Patrick's son is Dick Patrick. He's served as part-owner, president and alternate governor of the Washington Capitals since

1982, winning the Stanley Cup in 2018. Dick's son, Chris Patrick, has been working in the Washington front office since 2008 and got his name on the Cup along with his dad when Washington won it in 2018. That's a total of 13 Stanley Cup wins among seven family members. Lester, Frank and Craig Patrick are also members of the Hockey Hall of Fame.

Just Like Dad

Jeff Petry was traded twice during the summer of 2023. First he was sent from Pittsburgh to Montreal, and later from Montreal to Detroit. When he landed with the Red Wings, it was announced that Petry would wear number 46. That's the same number his father, Dan Petry, wore during most of his career as a major league pitcher with the Detroit Tigers.

Keep it in the Family

Scotty Bowman won the Stanley Cup a total of 14 times, including a record 9 times as an NHL coach. He won it five times in front-office roles. Scotty's son, Stan Bowman — who was named after the Stanley Cup when he was born in 1973 — won it three times as general manager of the Blackhawks. Scotty's nephew Steve Bowman got his name on the Stanley Cup as a scout with the Washington Capitals, meaning the Bowman family has its name on the Stanley Cup a total of 18 times. That's one more time than the Beliveau family, although in that case, all 17 wins are by one man! Legendary Montreal Canadiens star Jean Béliveau won the Stanley Cup 10 times as a player, then 7 times as a vice-president of the team.

Still, the record for Cup wins in a single family is 19, by the Richard brothers. Henri won the Cup a record 11 times as a player during his 20-year career with the Canadiens. His older brother, Maurice Richard, won it eight times in 18 years with Montreal.

Double Bill

When twin brothers Henrik and Daniel Sedin both entered the Hockey Hall of Fame in 2022, they became the ninth set of brothers to be named to the Hall as players, but the first to be inducted together in the same year. The twins spent their entire 17-season careers with the Vancouver Canucks from 2000 to 2018.

Did You Know?

Henrik and Daniel Sedin were inducted into the Hockey Hall of Fame along with long-time Canucks goalie Roberto Luongo. It marked the first time that three teammates were all enshrined at the same time.

Hockey Card History

The very first collectible cards depicting hockey scenes were issued back in 1879 and 1880. The first sets featuring professional hockey players came out in the winter of 1910. Like baseball cards of the same era, these early hockey cards came in packages of cigarettes. They showed star players from the National Hockey Association (forerunner of the NHL) on the front of the card and had information about the players on the back.

During the 1920s and '30s, food and candy companies began to make hockey cards. Production was discontinued during World War II but began again during the 1950s. These hockey cards were mainly produced for kids to collect, but since the 1990s, the hockey card hobby has become increasingly popular with adult collectors.

Hockey Card Mystery

More than 20 years after his NHL career ended, Wayne Gretzky was still setting records. In December of 2020, a 1979–80 O-Pee-Chee Wayne Gretzky rookie card sold for $1.65 million. It was the highest price ever paid for a hockey card . . . until a few months later, in May of 2021, when another Gretzky rookie card sold for $4.54 million. The condition of both cards had been rated "Gem Mint" — the highest rating possible.

In February of 2024, Heritage Auction in Dallas, Texas, sold a complete case of 1979–80 O-Pee-Chee hockey cards containing 16 sealed boxes that had never been opened. The case had been saved for more than 40 years by a family in Regina, Saskatchewan. It sold for just over $5 million. Most Gretzky rookie cards sell in the $1250 range. The case might contain dozens of them, though it's impossible to tell what their condition is. But since card experts say the value of the sealed boxes will go up, it would be a big risk to open them!

BY THE NUMBERS

There are several factors that make a hockey card valuable. Age is a factor. So is rarity or uniqueness. Some modern hockey cards are released in limited numbers to guarantee they will be rare. Still, the most important factor is often what kind of condition the card is in. These are the most valuable hockey cards ever sold:

CARD	DATE SOLD	AMOUNT*
1979–80 Wayne Gretzky rookie	May 2021	$4,540,000
1979–80 Wayne Gretzky rookie	Dec. 2020	$1,650,000
1966 Bobby Orr rookie	Feb. 2021	$330,000
2015 Connor McDavid rookie	June 2020	$184,000
2006–07 Dual Shield Gretzky/Lemieux	Oct. 2021	$113,000

*Canadian dollars

Trophy Tales

Though he had already signed with the Calgary Flames by then, Nazem Kadri got to celebrate with the Stanley Cup after winning it with Colorado in the 2022 Final. Kadri brought the trophy to his hometown of London, Ontario, where, for the first time ever, the trophy visited a mosque. Kadri started his day with the Cup at the London Muslim Mosque. "It's part of my background, it's part of my roots, it's part of who I am . . . I'm hoping that this inspires and motivates kids to pursue your dreams because I never thought this was possible," said Kadri. "I had some great support and people made me believe. If you believe, you can achieve."

Streakers

Mitch Marner was on a tear for the Toronto Maple Leafs early in the 2022–23 season. The star right-winger set a new team record when he scored points in 23 straight games from October 27 to December 13. Marner had 11 goals and 21 assists for 32 points during this streak. The old Leafs record of 18 straight games had been shared by Darryl Sittler and Eddie Olczyk. Marner's streak was the third-longest by any NHL player this century, trailing only Patrick Kane's 26 game-run (16 goals, 24 assists) in 2015–16 and Sidney Crosby's 25-game streak (26 goals, 24 assists) in 2010–11.

Did You Know?

On October 17, 2002, Bruins fan Tim Hurlbut climbed over the glass at an NHL game in Calgary wearing nothing but red socks on his feet. He slipped on the ice and knocked himself out!

BY THE NUMBERS

Only three players in NHL history have had a scoring streak last 30 games or more. Wayne Gretzky did it three times. Here's a look at the NHL's longest scoring streaks:

PLAYER, TEAM	STREAK	G	A	PTS	SEASON
Wayne Gretzky Edmonton	51 games	61	92	153	1983-84
Mario Lemieux Pittsburgh	46 games	39	64	103	1989-90
Wayne Gretzky Edmonton	39 games	33	75	108	1985-86
Wayne Gretzky Edmonton	30 games	24	52	76	1982-83
Mats Sundin Quebec	30 games	21	25	46	1992-93

NAME GAME
Team Names

Here are the stories behind the names of five teams that played in familiar NHL cities but are no longer part of the league. R.I.P:

The Montreal Maroons
The Maroons entered the NHL for the 1924–25 season. They were the third NHL team in Montreal, after the Canadiens and the Wanderers, who had both been part of the league for its inaugural season of 1917–18. Of course, the Canadiens still exist today, but the Wanderers didn't even make it through the first season! The new team had hoped to use the Wanderers name, but didn't receive permission from the original owners. Officially, they were known as the Montreal Professional Hockey Club, but people called them the Maroons because of the colour of their sweaters. Maroon is a brownish-red that looks almost purple.

The New York Americans

New York and Pittsburgh were the second and third American cities in the NHL after Boston, joining the league for the 1925–26 season. The New York team — which entered the NHL one year before the Rangers — wore star-spangled red, white and blue uniforms and called themselves the Americans for patriotic reasons.

The Pittsburgh Pirates

The Pittsburgh Yellow Jackets had won two straight American amateur hockey championships in 1923–24 and 1924–25. After the league they played in folded, the new owners of the team decided to join the NHL for the 1925–26 season. They brought plenty of Yellow Jackets players with them, but they didn't keep the name. The new team was named the Pirates in November of 1925, just like the city's baseball team, which had won the World Series in October. The hockey Pirates wore the same black-and-yellow colours as the Yellow Jackets. The baseball Pirates didn't adopt black and gold as their colours until 1948.

The Philadelphia Quakers

With the stock market crash in October of 1929, the steel industry in Pittsburgh, Pennsylvania was hurting. After a poor 1929–30 season, the owners of the Pittsburgh Pirates moved their team across the state to try their luck in Philadelphia. The team was renamed, becoming the Quakers. Pennsylvania is known as "the Quaker State" because it was founded in 1681 by William Penn, a leader of the Quaker religious movement. Sadly, the team lasted only one season. The NHL didn't return to Pittsburgh and Philadelphia until the 1967–68 season.

The St. Louis Eagles

The Great Depression hurt many NHL teams in the 1930s. Ottawa was the league's smallest market and found the going rough. Although the original Senators had won the Stanley Cup four times in the 1920s, the team was struggling so badly to sell tickets that in 1934 they moved to St. Louis. Unlike the Pittsburgh Pirates, the St. Louis hockey team didn't use the St. Louis baseball team's name, even though the Cardinals had just won the World Series. But they did stick with birds, naming the team the Eagles. Like the New York Americans, the choice was probably for patriotic reasons, since the bald eagle is the national bird of the United States. The Eagles lasted only one season. The NHL returned to St. Louis as the Blues in 1967-68. The Ottawa Senators didn't come back to the NHL until 1992.

Glass Houses

Back in the early days of indoor hockey, arenas didn't have anything on top of the boards to protect spectators from flying pucks. Fans sitting along the sides could lean right out over the ice, but they had to be careful! Not just pucks, but sticks and actual players would sometimes crash into them when they got checked.

Even in the early days of the NHL, a few arenas installed wire mesh above the boards, but only behind the net. Sometimes fans would reach through it and poke at the players or the referees if they didn't like a call.

Duquense Gardens, former home of the Pittsburgh Pirates, was the first arena to install protective glass above the boards. The Pittsburgh Plate Glass Company developed an "unbreakable" heat-tempered glass they called Herculite in 1937. It was purported to be up to five times stronger than regular plate glass. Herculite was tested at Duquense Gardens in 1940. Four years later, at least some was installed, likely in the areas behind the nets.

Herculite was used by the American military during World War II. After the war, an improved version of the glass was installed around the entire Duquesne Gardens ice surface before the start of the 1945–46 season. The innovation caught on . . . slowly. It wasn't until 2011 that all NHL arenas were using plexiglass instead.

DID YOU KNOW?

The Pittsburgh Plate Glass Company was founded in 1883 and it still exists today. These days it's known as PPG Industries and it makes paints, coatings and other specialty materials. The company still has a connection to hockey in Pittsburgh too. The Penguins have been playing their home games at PPG Paints Arena since the 2010–11 season.

NHL Glass

The NHL had only six teams when Duquesne Gardens first installed glass above the boards in 1944. So there were only six arenas too. The first NHL arena to install shatter resistant protective glass was Madison Square Garden in New York. It was added there at the start of the 1946–47 season. Like in Pittsburgh, the glass circled the entire ice surface ... except in front of the players' benches and in a few key spots where photographers took pictures.

The Montreal Forum also installed glass above the boards that season, but like the old wire mesh, only behind the nets. (Glass on the side boards wasn't added until the 1960–61 season.) Maple Leaf Gardens was a year behind the Forum. Toronto added it behind the nets for the 1947–48 season, but the Leafs were quicker than the Canadiens to put glass along the sides, which was done in 1958–59. When glass was added at the Boston Garden in 1948–49, it was put all around the rink — except in front of the players' benches.

At the Detroit Olympia, there were only wire screens protecting fans behind the nets until the 1958–59 season, when glass was finally put up. It extended all around the rink. The last of the NHL's Original Six teams to put in glass above the boards was the Chicago Black Hawks. They finally added glass at Chicago Stadium for the 1960–61 season. Finally, fans in all six NHL arenas had protection from flying pucks.

Hockey fans at Maple Leaf Gardens took matters into their own hands, using personal shields to protect their faces before glass was installed above the boards.

By the Rules

Section 1 in the NHL rule book covers the playing area. Rule 1, Part 3 talks about the boards and glass. It says this about the boards:

> *The rink shall be surrounded by a wall known as the "boards" which shall extend not less than forty inches (101.6 cm) and not more than forty-eight inches (121.9 cm) above the level of the ice surface. The ideal height of the boards above the ice surface shall be forty-two inches (106.7 cm).*

As for the glass:

> *Affixed to the boards and extending vertically shall be approved safety glass extending eight feet (2.4 meters) above the boards at each end of the rink and not less than five feet (1.5 meters) along both sides of the rink.*

The rules require there to be glass in front of the penalty boxes but not in front of the players' benches, although there is glass behind and beside the players' benches to shield and separate the players from the people sitting beside them. Netting is also hung above the glass to protect the fans in the areas behind the nets.

The Sin Bin

Penalties have been a part of hockey since the earliest rules were written, way back in the 1870s. Sometimes penalized players were charged money for their infractions, like getting a ticket for speeding!

In the early days, there wasn't always a place for players to go when they got sent off the ice to serve penalty minutes. Sometimes players sat atop the boards, waiting out their time. The first references to "the penalty box" began to appear in newspapers in 1907, but even when there were actual penalty boxes, most arenas had only one and both teams had to share it. In the NHL, an official sat in the penalty box between the players to make sure any trouble on the ice didn't carry over. It didn't always work.

In a game between Toronto and Montreal at Maple Leaf Gardens on October 30, 1963, Toronto's Bob Pulford and Terry Harper of the Canadiens got penalties for fighting and kept it up in the penalty box. After the game, Leafs president Stafford Smythe talked about partitioning the penalty box at Maple Leaf Gardens into two sections. Still, it seems the Canadiens did it first.

When the Chicago Black Hawks visited the Montreal Forum on November 7, 1963, not only was the penalty box split into two sections with two different entrances, there were painted signs screwed onto the boards by each entrance. Montreal's sign read "Good Guys/Bon Garçons." Chicago's said "Bad Guys/Mauvais Garçons." The signs didn't last very long. They were gone by the next game, but the separated penalty boxes with separate entrances stayed.

The new-style penalty boxes debuted at Maple Leaf Gardens two nights later when Toronto hosted Chicago on November 9, 1963. But the NHL didn't make it a rule to have two penalty boxes in every arena until the 1965–66 season. Even then, the rule said "it is preferable to have separate penalty benches for each team separated from each other." It wasn't until the 1972–73 season the NHL rule book stated: "separate penalty benches shall be provided for each team."

Knuckles Nilan

Chris Nilan was a right-winger and was known as a tough guy. He played 13 seasons in the NHL, from 1979 through 1992, mostly with the Montreal Canadiens but also with the New York Rangers and his hometown Boston Bruins. Nilan scored 21 goals for the Canadiens in 1984–85, and helped them win the Stanley Cup the following season. But Nilan was better known for throwing punches. That's how he got his nickname, "Knuckles." Nilan is one of just nine players in NHL history to top 3,000 penalty minutes, with 3,043 in his career. When he was playing for Boston, Nilan set an NHL record on March 31, 1991, with 10 penalties in a single game! After his career was over, Nilan was said to be interested in the bench or the door from the penalty box at the Montreal Forum when items were auctioned off after it closed in 1996. He didn't get either item.

DID YOU KNOW?

Chris Nilan holds the NHL record with 10 penalties in a single game, but his 42 penalty minutes that night are well short of the NHL penalty minutes record. Randy Holt of the Los Angeles Kings earned 69 penalty minutes on nine different penalties in a game against the Philadelphia Flyers on March 11, 1979.

BY THE NUMBERS

Auston Matthews ended the 2022–23 season with 299 career goals. He didn't waste much time getting to 300 goals once the 2023–24 season got under way. Matthews scored three times in Toronto's 6–5 shoot-out win over Montreal on opening night, October 11, 2023. By hitting the 300-goal plateau (and 301 and 302!) in just 482 games, he became the fastest Maple Leaf and the fastest American-born player to reach the milestone. Here are the all-time NHL players who have reached 300 goals in the fewest games, their citizenship and when they hit the mark:

PLAYER, CITIZENSHIP	GAMES	DATE
Wayne Gretzky, Canadian	350	December 13, 1983
Mario Lemieux, Canadian	368	April 2, 1989
Brett Hull, Canadian	377	April 12, 1992
Mike Bossy, Canadian	381	March 23, 1982
Jari Kurri, Finnish	441	April 6, 1986
Teemu Selanne, Finnish	464	February 27, 1999
Alex Ovechkin, Russian	473	April 5, 2011
Pavel Bure, Russian	478	January 22, 2000
Maurice Richard, Canadian	481	November 3, 1951
Auston Matthews, American	482	October 11, 2023

Life Goals: Goals

On March 27, 2023, in a game against the Arizona Coyotes, three different Edmonton Oilers had a chance to score their 300th goal. Only one did it that night, but the other two hit the milestone over the next two games.

Leon Draisaitl was the first. He scored late in the second period to help the Oilers beat the Coyotes 5–4 on the road in Arizona. Draisaitl reached the 300-goal plateau in his 630th career game. One night later, Evander Kane scored his 300th in Edmonton's 7–4 win against the Las Vegas Knights. Kane needed 846 games to accomplish the feat.

Next came Connor McDavid. With the Oilers back on home ice to face the Los Angeles Kings on March 30, 2023, McDavid scored early in the third period to help secure a 2–0 victory. He reached the milestone in 563 games and became the sixth player to score all his 300 goals with the Oilers, joining Draisaitl and Hockey Hall of Famers Wayne Gretzky, Jari Kurri, Glenn Anderson and Mark Messier.

Life Goals: Points

On January 3, 2023, when the Toronto Maple Leafs hosted the St. Louis Blues, both Auston Matthews and Mitch Marner entered the game with a chance to reach 500 points in their careers.

With 227 goals and 222 assists in his career, Matthews had 499 points. He hit the milestone with an assist early in the second period, and added a goal a few minutes later, but the Leafs lost 6–5. Still, by recording his 500th point in just his 445th game, Matthews set a new Leafs record for the fastest to 500.

Marner entered the game with 497 points (152 goals, 345 assists), but picked up only one assist that night. After another assist in Toronto's next game against Seattle, Marner scored against Detroit to reach 500 points on January 7, 2023. By reaching the milestone in his 467th game, Marner became the second-fastest Leaf to reach 500.

Did You Know?

Two teammates scoring their 500th point in the same game has happened only once before in NHL history. Chris Drury and Scott Gomez both reached the milestone with the New York Rangers on February 1, 2008.

BY THE NUMBERS

Auston Matthews and Mitch Marner became the 12th and 13th players in team history to score 500 points with the Maple Leafs. Here's a look at the seven fastest Toronto players to do it:

Auston Matthews	445 games
Mitch Marner	467 games
Mats Sundin	495 games
Rick Vaive	495 games
Darryl Sittler	517 games
Frank Mahovlich	591 games
Borje Salming	597 games

100-Year Hat Tricks

When Auston Matthews followed up his three goals on opening night with three more in the Leafs' second game of the 2023–24 season, he became just the fifth player in NHL history to begin a season with back-to-back hat tricks and only the second in over 100 years. The other four players to accomplish this feat were Joe Malone, Cy Denneny and Reg Noble, back in the NHL's first season of 1917–18, and Alex Ovechkin, who did it 100 years later in 2017–18.

Matthews scores his hat trick goal against goalie Filip Gustavsson of the Minnesota Wild during the third period on October 14, 2023.

Unlikely X-Men

Defenceman Arber Xhekaj is the first player in NHL history whose last name starts with the letter "X." He has an unusual hockey story, even beyond his unique last name, which is pronounced Jack-Eye.

In 1994, Xhekaj's father came to Canada as a refugee from Kosovo and settled in Hamilton, Ontario. Xhekaj's mom had also just moved to Canada, from Czechia, with a single suitcase in hand. They soon met, married and went on to raise four children in Hamilton.

Xhekaj stands 1.93 metres tall (6 ft. 4 in.) and weighs 108 kilograms (238 lbs.), but back in his Hamilton Huskies minor hockey days, he was smaller than many other players. To improve his chances of getting drafted into the OHL, Xhekaj also played for Toronto and Mississauga even though it meant a lot of commutes from Hamilton.

No OHL team drafted Xhekaj, but after a year of playing Junior B hockey, he earned a spot with the Kitchener Rangers in 2018–19. When

COVID-19 wiped out the 2020–21 OHL season, some of his teammates played overseas or booked private ice and trainers to stay in shape. Xhekaj stayed in Hamilton and got a job at Costco. But he still dreamed of the NHL.

Xhekaj wasn't drafted by the NHL in the 2021 Draft that summer either, but in the fall, he signed a free-agent contract with the Montreal Canadiens. The Canadiens sent him back to the OHL, where he played the season and helped his hometown Hamilton Bulldogs reach the finals of the 2022 Memorial Cup.

Finally, on October 12, 2022, Xhekaj made his NHL debut with Canadiens in their 3–2 winning home opener against the Toronto Maple Leafs. In all, Xhekaj played 51 games in his rookie season, with five goals and eight assists. The Canadiens then selected his younger brother, Florian Xhekaj, in the fourth round of the 2023 NHL Draft with the 101st pick overall. So there may be another member of the X-Men playing in the NHL one day!

NAME GAME
Modern Edition

When Arber Xhekaj was playing junior hockey, his teammates called him "Al" because "Arber" sounds the same as the last name of legendary New York Islanders coach Al Arbour. Xhekaj is also known as "Wi-Fi" because his unusual last name is similar to the the default passwords used for internet access.

NAME GAME
Team Names

The Kitchener Rangers franchise began in 1947 as the Guelph Biltmore Mad Hatters, named after their local sponsor, the Biltmore Hat Company of Guelph, Ontario. In those days, junior teams were farm clubs for the NHL, and the Guelph team was a farm team of the New York Rangers. When the team moved to Kitchener in 1963, the Mad Hatters used the Rangers nickname and have continued to use it even though NHL sponsorship of junior teams ended in 1967.

The Next Next One

Ever since people started calling Wayne Gretzky "the Great One" in the early 1980s, many top NHL prospects have been dubbed "the Next One." Eric Lindros, Paul Kariya, Sidney Crosby, John Tavares and Connor McDavid all had the tag attached to them. Now there's another on the list: Connor Bedard. Bedard was born in North Vancouver on January 17, 2005. He played for the West Van Academy bantam team in the Canadian Sport School Hockey League (CSSHL) as a 13-year-old in 2018–19. That season he had 64 goals and 24 assists for 88 points in just 30 games, leading all bantam-aged players. Bedard was still bantam-aged the next season, but he played with the West Van prep team in the under-18 division of the CSSHL. Again he led this division in scoring, this time with 43 goals and 41 assists for 84 points in 36 games.

At 14, Bedard — who would turn 15 in July of 2020 — was eligible for the 2020 Western Hockey League's Bantam Draft (now called the Prospects Draft). However, WHL rules say that 15-year-old players can play only five games in the league before their minor hockey team's season is over. Bedard was so good, the decision was made to grant him exceptional player status, which would allow him to play the entire WHL season as a 15-year-old. It seemed a given when the Regina Pats made Bedard the first pick in the 2020 WHL Draft.

COVID-19 cut short the 2020–21 WHL season, so Bedard played only 15 games. He still had 12 goals and 16 assists to lead all rookies with 28 points. In his first full season, in 2021–22, Bedard had 51 goals and 49 assists for 100 points in 62 games, which ranked him fourth in the league behind three players who were all at least two years older than he was. In 2022–23, Bedard led the WHL with an amazing 71 goals and 72 assists for 143 points in just 57 games played. No one else in the league had more than 107 points and no one else had more than 50 goals.

No one was surprised when the Chicago Blackhawks made Connor Bedard the first pick in the 2023 NHL Draft. In his first game for Chicago, in a pre-season prospects tournament on September 16, 2023, Bedard had three goals and an assist in a 5–0 victory over St. Louis. In his first true pre-season game, also against the Blues, Bedard had two assists to lead the Blackhawks to a 2–1 victory.

On October 10, 2023, Bedard played his first regular-season NHL game on the opening night of the 2023–24 season. Playing against Sidney Crosby and the Pittsburgh Penguins, Bedard was excited to be facing one of his hockey heroes. "He's such a good role model for everyone," said Bedard. "He's been in the spotlight for almost 20 years now and seems to have handled it so well." Crosby also had a few words about the new player "[Bedard] was a guy who is more than ready at this point. He's been dealing with the expectations for a while. I think he's just ready to finally start."

Bedard faced Crosby on the opening face-off, but lost the draw. Still, it was a pretty good start for hockey's newest hero. Though Crosby scored a goal to help Pittsburgh jump out to a 2–0 lead, Bedard helped set up Chicago's first goal for his first NHL point. The Blackhawks went on to rally for a 4–2 victory, and Bedard led all Chicago forwards with 21 minutes and 29 seconds of ice time. When asked what he would remember most about his NHL debut, Bedard said, "Winning, for sure." The next night, October 11, 2023, the Blackhawks lost 3–1 to the Boston Bruins, but Bedard scored his first regular-season NHL goal.

NAME GAME
Classic Edition

Angela James played at the highest level of women's hockey from 1980 until 1998. She won eight scoring titles and six MVP awards in various different leagues, leading to her nickname, "the Wayne Gretzky of Women's Hockey."

Exceptional Status

Connor Bedard was the first WHL player to be granted exceptional player status to play in the league as a 15-year-old. Exceptional status is granted to a highly skilled young player whose hockey development is likely to be significantly improved by playing major junior hockey rather than staying in their designated age division.

Before Bedard, six other players had been given the honour in the other Canadian major junior leagues. John Tavares (2005), Aaron Ekblad (2011), Connor McDavid (2012), Sean Day (2013) and Shane Wright (2019) were granted early entry into the Ontario Hockey League, while Joe Veleno (2015) got the same status in the Quebec Major Junior Hockey League.

Since Bedard, exceptional status was granted by the OHL to Michael Misa in 2022. He was selected first overall by the Saginaw Spirit in the 2022 OHL Draft. Exceptional status was granted *again* by the WHL in 2024 for Landon DuPont, who was drafted first overall by the Everett Silvertips.

Female Firsts

At the 2022 WHL Prospects Draft, the Vancouver Giants selected 15-year-old defenceman Chloe Primerano with the 268th choice. Primerano was the first female player ever drafted into the WHL. She's also the first female skater to be drafted by any Canadian major junior team.

Primerano was selected after playing the 2021–22 season with the Burnaby Winter Club's under-15 prep boys team in the Canadian Sport School Hockey League. She went to training camp with the Vancouver Giants in September of 2022, but played the 2022–23 season with the under-18 RINK Hockey Academy female team in Kelowna, British Columbia. Primerano led all defencemen in the CSSHL in scoring with 20 goals and 28 assists for 48 points in 30 games that season. She also represented British Columbia in women's hockey at the 2023 Canada Winter Games in Prince Edward Island, where she was first in the tournament in scoring with 5 goals and 9 assists for 14 points in six games — and led

B.C. to the gold medal. In the 2023 WHL Draft, the Portland Winterhawks selected another female player when they chose goalie Morgan Stickney with the 215th pick. The only female players drafted to date by teams in the OHL and the QMJHL are also goalies. There's Charline Labonté (Acadie-Bathurst, 1999: 174th pick) and Jenny Lavigne (Rimouski, 2002: 213th) in the Quebec league and Taya Currie (Sarnia, 2021: 267th) in Ontario.

BY THE NUMBERS

Here's a look at the single-season scoring records in Canadian major junior hockey:

LEAGUE	PLAYER	SEASON	GP	G	A	PTS
QMJHL	Mario Lemieux	1983–84	70	133	149	282
WHL	Rob Brown	1986–87	62	76	136	212
OHL	Bobby Smith	1977–78	61	69	123	192

Lemieux and Brown were both 18 years old when they set their league records. Smith was 19. Connor Bedard was only 17 years old in his final junior season in 2022–23. Here's how he stacks up against other scoring greats in their 17-year-old seasons:

LEAGUE	PLAYER	SEASON	GP	G	A	PTS
QMJHL	Mario Lemieux	1982–83	66	84	100	184
OHL	Wayne Gretzky	1977–78	63	70	112	182
QMJHL	Sidney Crosby	2004–05	62	66	102	168
OHL	Eric Lindros	1990–91	57	71	78	149
WHL	Connor Bedard	2022–23	57	71	72	143
OHL	Connor McDavid	2014–15	47	44	76	120

Let There Be Light

Early hockey games were played outdoors, on frozen lakes and rivers, by the sun or the moon. The first public display of a hockey game indoors took place in Montreal's Victoria Skating Rink on March 3, 1875. The Victoria rink had large windows to let in daylight, and 500 gas-jet fixtures set in coloured glass globes provided light at night. These were later replaced with electric light bulbs. Many stories say the Victoria rink was the first building in Canada with electric light. Rinks in smaller cities in this early era were sometimes lit with oil lamps.

When Maple Leaf Gardens opened in Toronto in 1931, its rink was illuminated with more than 100 specially made 1,000-watt lamps. At the time, a typical lamp would use one or two 60- or 100-watt bulbs. Still, the Gardens, even lit with over 100,000 watts, would seem pretty dull compared to today.

During the 1950s and '60s, many smaller rinks began changing from incandescent lighting to fluorescent lamp lighting. Fluorescents were bright and far cheaper to operate, even if they were prone to buzzing and flickering. Rinks that could afford to also used high-intensity discharge lighting — which is bright, but expensive. These days, many NHL rinks use LED lights. The more natural-looking LED lights make the ice appear whiter and the other colours in arenas more visually appealing, especially when viewed on a screen. They're also more energy efficient, which is much better for the environment.

Junior Achievement

Technically, the World Junior championship (WJC) is called the U20 World Championship, because it's a tournament for players who are under 20 years old. But if you're watching the games on TV, you'll often hear the announcers say it's a tournament for 19-year-olds, as that's the how old most of the players are. But when Connor Bedard made the Canadian World Junior team for the first time in the 2021–22 season, he was only 16 years old. The only other Canadian players to make that team at 16 were Wayne Gretzky (1978), Eric Lindros (1990), Jay Bouwmeester (2000), Jason Spezza (2000), Sidney Crosby (2004) and Connor McDavid (2014).

Bedard had four goals and four assists for eight points in seven games to help Canada win gold at the World Junior Championship in 2022. The tournament was played in August that year, after being postponed due to COVID-19 in December. Bedard had played two games before the cancellation. He had one assist in a 6–3 win in his first game, and then exploded with four goals in an 11–2 win over Austria in the next.

Bedard was even more amazing as a 17-year-old at the 2022–23 WJC. Not only did he lead Canada to gold again, he was named the tournament MVP and set all sorts of scoring records. With 23 points (9 goals, 14 assists) in just seven games, he broke the previous Canadian scoring record of 18 points in one tournament, shared by Dale McCourt (1977) and Bryden Schenn (2011), as well as the old record of 12 assists. By doing it all at the age of 17, Bedard also broke the previous tournament record for points by a 17-year-old, set by Jaromir Jágr, who hit 18 points back in 1990.

In his two years at the WJC, Bedard totaled 36 points (17 goals and 19 assists), breaking the previous Canadian record, held by Eric Lindros in points (31) and Jordan Eberle in goals (14).

Awesome Auston

On February 21, 2024, Auston Matthews scored his 50th goal of the season (and his 51st) in the Leafs' 6–3 win over the Coyotes. The game was played in Arizona, not far from Matthews' hometown of Scottsdale. Matthews reached the 50-goal plateau in just his 54th game of the season and the Leafs' 55th of the year. It was the fewest games for anyone to hit the milestone since Mario Lemieux scored 50 goals in 50 games in 1995–96, though he was well short of Wayne Gretzky's record of 50 goals in 39 games, set in 1981–82. Matthews finished the year with 69 goals, tying Mario Lemieux from 1995–96 for the most goals in one season since Teemu Selanne and Alexander Mogilny both scored 76 in 1992–93.

McDavid McMagic

Connor McDavid set career highs during the 2022–23 season with 64 goals, 89 assists and 153 points. His 153 points were the most by any player in one season since Mario Lemieux had 161 in 1995–96. For McDavid, it was the fifth time he'd won the Art Ross Trophy as the NHL scoring leader in eight seasons in the league. Only five other players have won the trophy five times or more: Wayne Gretzky (10), Gordie Howe (6), Mario Lemieux (6), Phil Esposito (5) and Jaromir Jágr (5).

McDavid was also just the fifth player in NHL history to lead the league in goals, assists and points in the same season. The others were Howie Morenz in 1927–28, Gordie Howe in 1950–51, Phil Esposito in 1972–73 and Wayne Gretzky, who did it five times in six seasons between 1981 and 1987. Mario Lemieux also did it in 1988–89, although Lemieux tied Gretzky for the NHL lead in assists that season while leading outright in goals and points.

In 2023–24, McDavid and Nikita Kucherov of the Tampa Bay Lightning both finished the season with 100 assists. They were only the fourth and fifth players in NHL history to reach that milestone, joining Bobby Orr (102 in 1970–71), Mario Lemieux (114 in 1988–89) and Wayne Gretzky, who did it an astounding 11 times!

NAME GAME
Classic Edition

Aurele Joliat starred with the Montreal Canadiens for 16 seasons from 1922 to 1936. Joliat enjoyed nine seasons as a top-10 scorer, won the Hart Trophy as NHL MVP for the 1932–33 season, and was a Stanley Cup champion in 1924, 1930 and 1931. At 1.7 metres (5 ft., 7 in.), Joliat was only a little bit short for a player of this era, but he weighed only 62 kg (136 lb.), which makes him one of the smallest players in NHL history. No surprise, then, that Joliat was known as "the Mighty Atom" and "the Little Giant."

DID YOU KNOW?

April 8, 2023, was the busiest day in NHL history to that date. With 16 games on the schedule, all 32 teams were in action on the same night for the first time ever. Game results and start times (Eastern Standard time) that day were:

TEAMS, SCORES	START TIME
Carolina 3 at Buffalo 4	12:30 p.m.
Pittsburgh 5 at Detroit 1	1:00 p.m.
Vegas 1 at Dallas 2	3:30 p.m.
Edmonton 6 at San Jose 1	4:00 p.m.
Anaheim 4 at Arizona 5	5:30 p.m.
Florida 4 at Washington 2	7:00 p.m.
Montreal 1 at Toronto 7	7:00 p.m.
NY Rangers 4 at Columbus 0	7:00 p.m.
Nashville 0 at Winnipeg 2	7:00 p.m.
Tampa Bay 4 at Ottawa 7	7:00 p.m.
Philadelphia 0 at NY Islanders 4	7:30 p.m.
St. Louis 3 at Minnesota 5	8:00 p.m.
New Jersey 1 at Boston 2	8:00 p.m.
Calgary 2 at Vancouver 3	10:00 p.m.
Chicago 3 at Seattle 7	10:00 p.m.
Colorado 4 at Los Angeles 3	10:30 p.m.

A Dollar Well Spent

Ray Sheppard played with six different NHL teams in a 13-year career from 1987 to 2000. He scored 38 goals as a rookie with the Buffalo Sabres in 1987–88, but struggled over the next two seasons. In the summer of 1991, Sheppard was sold to the New York Rangers for just one dollar! He bounced back with 24 goals for the Rangers in 1990–91, and three years later, he scored a career-high 52 goals for the Detroit Red Wings.

During the summer of 1993, Detroit bought Kris Draper from the Winnipeg Jets. The price of that deal was also one dollar. Draper had played just 20 games over three seasons with the Jets, but he became a key player for the Red Wings. Used mostly as a checker who shut down other team's top stars, Draper played 17 seasons in Detroit between 1993 and 2011. He won the Frank J. Selke Trophy as the NHL's best defensive forward for the 2003–04 season and helped the Red Wings to four Stanley Cup victories.

MASCOT MAYHEM

Seattle didn't have a mascot during its first NHL season of 2021–22. During that season, the Kraken promoted a "team dog" named Davy Jones after the mythical pirate. This Davy Jones was a husky mix puppy who socialized with fans at home games as he trained to be a therapy dog.

An official Kraken mascot was finally introduced at a pre-season game before the team's second season of 2022–23. His name is Buoy (pronounced Boo-ee), like a floating navigational device, but Buoy the mascot is actually a troll. He was inspired by the Fremont Troll, a statue of a troll under a bridge in the Fremont neighbourhood of Seattle. Buoy's wavy blue troll hair is said to be inspired by the waves of Puget Sound and the flow of a hockey game. Now that Seattle has a mascot, the New York Rangers are the only NHL team without one.

Skate Debate

The earliest skates date back about 5,000 years. The blades were made from the shin bones of animals. Skaters made holes in the bone and threaded leather straps through the holes to tie the blades to their feet. People didn't skate for fun back then. It was a way to move around quickly — mainly to hunt for food — in cold-weather countries.

Metal skate blades date back to around the 1400s, but it wasn't until the late 1800s and early 1900s that strap-on skates gave way to boots with the screwed-in blades. The new skates allowed those early hockey players to stop, start and change direction more easily.

Metal blades glide over the ice with little friction. Scientists used to think that the pressure of a skater's body weight melted the top layer of ice and made it slippery, allowing blades to slide across it. However, it's now believed ice is always slippery because the molecules in its top layer behave like liquid water.

60-Goal Seasons

When Connor McDavid scored 64 goals for Edmonton in 2022–23 a year after Auston Matthews got 60 for Toronto, it was the first time there were 60-goal scorers in back-to-back seasons for almost 30 years. But starting in the 1980–81 season, it happened 14 times in a row! Boston's David Pastrnak also scored 61 goals in 2022–23. This was the first time that two players hit 60 in the same year since 1995–96, when Pittsburgh's Mario Lemieux and Jaromir Jágr scored 69 and 62, respectively.

100-Point Trios

With Connor McDavid (153), Leon Draisaitl (128) and Ryan Nugent Hopkins (104) all topping 100 points for the Edmonton Oilers in 2022–23, they became the first trio of teammates to hit 100 points in one season since Mario Lemieux (161), Jaromir Jágr (149) and Ron Francis (119) accomplished this with Pittsburgh in 1995–96.

Hockey Math: 4 x 100

Three different teams in NHL history have had four players score 100 points in a season. The first was the Boston Bruins in 1970–71, with Phil Esposito (152), Bobby Orr (139), Johnny Bucyk (116) and Ken Hodge (105). The most recent was the 1992–93 Pittsburgh Penguins with Mario Lemieux (160), Kevin Stevens (111), Rick Tocchet (109) and Ron Francis (100).

The Edmonton Oilers have boasted four 100-point players in a season three different times. In 1982–83, it was Wayne Gretzky (196), Mark Messier (106), Glenn Anderson (104) and Jari Kurri (104). In 1983–84, it was Gretzky (205), Paul Coffey (126), Kurri (113) and Messier (101). In 1985–86, it was Gretzky with an NHL record–breaking 215 points along with Coffey (138), Kurri (131) and Anderson (102).

Hockey Math: 4 x 200

Wayne Gretzky is the only player in NHL history to top 200 points in a regular season, and he did it an amazing four times! In addition to the 1982–83 and 1985–86 seasons already listed, Gretzky also had 212 points in 1981–82 and 208 points in 1984–85.

BY THE NUMBERS

These players have had the most seasons with 60 or more goals in NHL history:

PLAYER	60 GOALS	TOTAL SEASONS
Mike Bossy	5 times	10 seasons
Wayne Gretzky	5 times	20 seasons
Mario Lemieux	4 times	17 seasons
Phil Esposito	4 times	18 seasons
Brett Hull	3 times	19 seasons
Pavel Bure	2 times	12 seasons
Jari Kurri	2 times	17 seasons
Steve Yzerman	2 times	22 seasons
Auston Matthews*	2 times	8 seasons

*still active

Four Fastest Goals

Tage Thompson scored five goals in a game for the Buffalo Sabres in a 9–4 win over the Columbus Blue Jackets on December 7, 2022. He scored the first four of his five goals that night in the first period.

Only Joe Malone of the Hamilton Tigers scored his four goals faster than Thompson, and that was more than 100 years ago! On February 23, 1921, Malone scored four times by the 8:45 mark of the first period in a 7–4 win over the Toronto St. Pats. Thompson took until the 16:40 mark.

Since Malone's speedy goals, two other players have scored four times in the first period: Grant Mulvey for Chicago by the 18:31 mark in a 9–5 win over St. Louis on February 3, 1982, and Peter Bondra for Washington at 18:56 in a 6–3 win over Tampa Bay on February 5, 1994. Mulvey, Bondra and Thompson went on to score a fifth goal in their games, but Malone did not.

All Hail Cale!

The Colorado Avalanche made Cale Makar the fourth choice overall in the 2017 NHL Draft. Makar spent the next two seasons playing hockey at the University of Massachusetts. Two days after winning the Hobey Baker Award as the top player in U.S. college hockey for the 2018–19 season, Makar signed his first contract with the Colorado Avalanche.

The next day, on April 15, 2019, Makar made his NHL debut. It was a playoff game for Colorado against Calgary, and he scored a goal in the first period to help spark a 6–2 victory that gave the Avalanche the series. It was their first playoff victory in 11 years, and Makar was the first defenceman ever to score a playoff goal in his NHL debut.

From there, things just kept getting better! In 2019–20, his first full NHL season, Makar won the Calder Trophy as rookie of the year. In his second season, he was a First-Team All-Star and finished second in voting for the Norris Trophy as the league's best defenceman.

In the 2021–22 season, Makar set a franchise record for a defencemen with 28 goals and 86 points. This time, he not only won the Norris, he helped lead Colorado to the Stanley Cup and also won the Conn Smythe Trophy as the playoff MVP.

Makar wasted no time getting his 200th regular-season point — a goal — in his 195th game. He is the first defenceman in NHL history to reach the mark that fast, surpassing Hockey Hall of Famer Sergei Zubov, who did it in 207 games.

Makar got his 200th point on November 21, 2022, in the Avalanche's 3–2 win against the Dallas Stars.

Trophy Tales

The Stanley Cup has had its adventures. It's been to the top of mountains and the bottom of swimming pools. It's been on beaches and on boats. In all its travels, the Stanley Cup sometimes gets dropped and dented, but it sure didn't take long for the Stanley Cup to suffer some damage after the Colorado Avalanche beat the Tampa Bay Lightning to win it in 2022.

Mere minutes after the Cup was presented, Nicolas Aube-Kubel of the Avalanche was skating with it toward centre ice where his teammates were gathering for the traditional victory photo. As he was leaning in to put it down, Kubel took a tumble and bashed the base on the ice.

"I don't even know if they had it five minutes and there's a dent at the bottom already," said Phil Pritchard, the Hockey Hall of Fame's Keeper of the Cup. "I guess it's a new record today, five minutes into the presentation . . . It's the first time it's ever happened on the ice."

MASCOT MAYHEM

Iceburgh, the mascot of the Pittsburgh Penguins, debuted in 1992–93. Iceburgh looks like a Muppet version of a king penguin, but Pittsburgh used to have a real penguin as its mascot. At the start of the team's second season, in 1968–69, they introduced Penguin Pete, who was a real penguin on loan from the local zoo. Penguin Pete was even taught to skate and had his own custom-made blades.

Sadly, Penguin Pete was not properly cared for by his zoo handlers and died just a few weeks into the season. The Penguins introduced a new mascot for the 1971–72 season and called him Re-Pete. But times were changing, and performing animals were no longer welcomed in the way the original Pete had been. So for 20 years, Pittsburgh had no mascot. When a new one was finally introduced, there was already a costumed penguin named Pete at Youngstown State University in Ohio. The name Iceburgh was chosen in a name-the-mascot contest.

DID YOU KNOW?

As an 18-year-old rookie with Pittsburgh in 2005–06, Sidney Crosby scored 39 goals. In his 18th season, in 2022–23, he scored 33 goals for them, making him the first player in NHL history to have a 30-goal season as an 18-year-old and again at the age of 35 or older.

Chips off the Old Blocks

Quinn Hughes was named captain of the Vancouver Canucks on September 11, 2023. He became the 15th captain in team history — the third defenceman to hold that honour.

Hughes was born in Orlando, Florida, but he grew up in Toronto. His family moved there in 2006. He comes from a hockey background. His mother, Ellen Weinberg-Hughes, won a silver medal with the U.S. team at the 1992 Women's World Championship. His father, Jim Hughes, played in college and went on to be an assistant coach with the Boston Bruins and then director of player development for the Toronto Maple Leafs. Quinn's younger brothers, Jack and Luke, were each selected by the New Jersey Devils in the NHL Draft, with Jack the number-one pick in 2019 and Luke number four in 2021. Quinn had been the seventh pick in the 2018 draft.

BY THE NUMBERS

With two assists on March 4, 2023, Quinn Hughes reached the 200-assist milestone faster than any defenceman in NHL history. Hughes needed 263 games to get there. But he didn't hold the record for long! On November 18, 2023, Cale Makar picked up three assists, making them the 199th, 200th and 201st career assists in just his 254th game. Here's a look at the 10 fastest defencemen to reach 200 assists:

PLAYER	GAMES PLAYED
Cale Makar	254
Quinn Hughes	263
Brian Leetch	264
Bobby Orr	271
Gary Suter	276
Sergei Zubov	279
Paul Coffey	287
Al MacInnis	288
Denis Potvin	295
Mark Howe	298

Trading Talent

Erik Karlsson was chosen by the Ottawa Senators as the 15th pick in the first round of the 2008 NHL Draft. He entered the NHL in 2009–10. With blazing speed and a powerful shot, Karlsson quickly became a star as a high-scoring defenceman. He was barely 22 years old when he first won the Norris Trophy in 2012 as the NHL's best defenceman, making him the youngest Norris Trophy winner since Bobby Orr in 1968. Karlsson won the trophy again in 2015. After that, injuries began to slow him down.

In 2018, Ottawa traded Karlsson to San Jose. Injuries still plagued him, and he wasn't truly healthy again until the 2022–23 season. That year, Karlsson had 25 goals and 76 assists for 101 points, which made him the first defenceman to reach the 100-point plateau since Hall of Famer Brian Leetch scored 102 for the New York Rangers in 1991–92.

Karlsson finished his big season by winning the Norris Trophy for the third time. Still, San Jose traded him to the Pittsburgh Penguins before the 2023–24 season. This was the first time a defenceman was traded fresh off winning the Norris Trophy since the Montreal Canadiens sent future Hockey Hall of Famer Doug Harvey to the New York Rangers after the 1960–61 season. That was the sixth time Harvey had won the Norris. He won it again in 1961–62 with the Rangers. Only Bobby Orr has won it more, with eight wins.

Goalie Life Goals

Gary Smith was a backup goalie for the Toronto Maple Leafs when he was called in to replace the starter early in the first period of a game in Montreal on December 21, 1966. A few minutes later, Smith stopped a shot, dropped the puck, and began stickhandling up the ice. He got almost to the centre red line before he passed it. A few days later, the NHL announced a new rule preventing goalies from carrying the puck past centre. Today, that's rule #27.7 in the NHL rule book.

In a game against the New York Rangers on November 16, 1997, Colorado goalie Patrick Roy was given an unsportsmanlike conduct penalty when he carried the puck across centre. Why did he do it? "I didn't know the rule," Roy said, "[and] it was my dream to deke Wayne Gretzky once in my life."

Score-y Perry

Corey Perry set a unique record when he became the first player in NHL history to score a goal with four different teams in the Stanley Cup Finals: the Ducks, the Stars, the Canadiens and the Lightning. Perry won the Stanley Cup with the Anaheim Ducks in 2007. In 2020, he played in the Stanley Cup Finals for Dallas against Tampa Bay, but lost it that year. In 2021, he was with the Montreal Canadiens, and lost to Tampa once again in the Stanley Cup Finals. In 2022, Perry was with Tampa Bay when they reached the finals for the third straight year, but this time they lost to Colorado.

Perry accomplished another unique feat. He's the only NHL player to score a regular-season goal and a Stanley Cup goal in September. Perry scored for Anaheim on September 30, 2007, when the Ducks opened the NHL season with games against Los Angeles in London, England. He scored for Dallas against Tampa Bay on September 25 and 26, 2020, when COVID-19 delayed the start of the playoffs until August.

Jack of All Leagues

The Stanley Cup is actually 25 years older than the NHL is, and in the NHL's first 10 seasons, the league winner played against the champions of other leagues to win it. Back in the 1910s and '20s, future Hockey Hall of Famer Jack Walker scored Stanley Cup goals with four different teams: in 1911 with Port Arthur of the New Ontario Hockey League, in 1914 with the Toronto Blueshirts of the National Hockey Association, three times with the Seattle Metropolitans of the Pacific Coast Hockey Association (1917, 1919 and 1920) and in 1925 with the Victoria Aristocrats of the Western Canada Hockey League. Walker won the Cup with Toronto in 1914, Seattle in 1917 and Victoria in 1925. Victoria was the last non-NHL team to win it.

First Nations First

Brigette Lacquette grew up in the remote community of Mallard, Manitoba. Her father is from the O-Chi-Chak Ko Sipi First Nation of Manitoba, while her mother is from the Cote First Nation in Saskatchewan. Lacquette started skating when she was four years old, and knew she wanted to play hockey by the time she was five. Mallard is so small that there aren't any community hockey rinks . . . so Lacquette's dad built one in their backyard.

Shortly after her 21st birthday, she was selected to play defence for the Canadian national women's team at the 2013 Four Nations Cup, helping Canada win the gold medal. Lacquette went on to represent Canada at the Women's World Championships in 2015 and 2016.

Then, in 2018, she made the Canadian team that competed at PyeongChang, South Korea, which made her the first Indigenous woman to play hockey for Canada at the Olympics.

Indigenous NHL

Fred Sasakamoose is recognized as the first Indigenous player with Treaty status in the NHL. Sasakamoose played 11 games with Chicago during the 1953–54 NHL season. Treaty status refers to a person being registered under the Indian Act of Canada. Treaty Indians are people belonging to a First Nations band that has signed a treaty with the government.

Although he isn't officially recognized by the NHL, some sources say that Henry Elmer "Buddy" Maracle, Haudenosaunee of the Six Nations, may have preceded Sasakamoose. In the 1930-31 season he played 11 games with the New York Rangers, and his hockey career spanned 30 years.

And before Maracle played in the NHL, there was Clarence "Taffy" Abel. His mother was Ojibwe and his father was white, so Taffy did not have status, according to the government's policies at that time. He played with New York and Chicago from 1926 to 1934 and won a silver medal in men's hockey at the very first Winter Olympics, held in 1924.

Great Gretzky Record Breaker

In Wayne Gretzky's career, he had 894 goals in the NHL regular season, plus another 122 in playoff games. Before joining the NHL, Gretzky had 46 regular-season goals in the World Hockey Association, plus 10 goals in the playoffs. He also scored 26 goals in major international tournaments. Add it all up, and Gretzky had 1,098 professional goals, a record that stood for 24 years. But on February 5, 2023, when Jaromir Jágr scored for the Kladno Knights in the Czech Extralinga, he broke Gretzky's record. In Jágr's NHL career, he had 766 regular-season goals and 78 playoff goals. Add to that his 93 goals in the Kontinental Hockey League in Russia, 107 goals in Czech league play, plus 55 goals in major international tournaments. By the end of the 2023-24 season, he had made a wildly impressive 1,101 goals in his professional career.

Cool in Kladno

Jaromir Jágr grew up in Kladno, Czechia, and has owned the team there since the 2011–12 season. He bought it when he was still playing in the NHL. Jágr ended his NHL career in 2018, but has kept playing in Kladno since the 2018–19 season. There were a few times over the years when Jágr thought he'd probably retire, but he kept returning to action to help out the team when other players got injured. The 2023–24 campaign marked his 36th professional season.

DID YOU KNOW?

Players need to be retired for at least three years before they are named to the Hockey Hall of Fame in Toronto, so Jágr isn't in it — yet. However, he was inducted into the International Ice Hockey Federation Hall of Fame in 2024.

52 Is the New 40

Mark Giordano celebrated his 40th birthday on October 3, 2023. When he lined up on defence with the Toronto Maple Leafs in their 2023–24 season opener against Montreal eight days later, Giordano was the oldest active player in the NHL and the 95th player in league history to play after turning 40.

During the 2023–24 season, Jaromir Jágr broke Gordie Howe's record to become the oldest player to play regularly for a professional hockey team. When Jágr suited up for Kladno on April 18, 2024, he was 52 years and 63 days old. By scoring a goal that night, he set another record: as the oldest goal scorer in a professional game. Howe scored his last goal when he was 52 years and 9 days old. He retired 2 days later.

Building a Legacy

Willie O'Ree played only 45 games over parts of two NHL seasons during a pro career that lasted more than 20 seasons between 1956 and 1979. When O'Ree played his first NHL game, on January 18, 1958, for the Boston Bruins against the Canadiens in Montreal, he became the first Black player in NHL history. In 1998, the NHL hired O'Ree as the Director of Youth Development for its diversity task force. In 2018, O'Ree was recognized for his years of service to the game when he was inducted as a Builder into the Hockey Hall of Fame.

In 2022, the Hockey Hall of Fame honoured Herb Carnegie with induction as a Builder. Carnegie was a star player in various pro and senior amateur leagues from 1938 through 1954. Playing in Timmins, Ontario, in 1941–42, Carnegie played on an all-Black line with his brother, Ossie Carnegie, and Manny McIntyre. Herb went to training camp with the New York Rangers in 1948, but, like many other Black players, did not get a fair chance at the NHL.

They offered him a $2,700 contract to play in their minor league — less than he was making in Canada and less than white players in the league were offered.

After his hockey career ended, Carnegie enjoyed success in the investment industry. He also founded Future Aces, one of Canada's first hockey schools, in 1955. He not only taught hockey skills, but life lessons too. The Herbert H. Carnegie Future Aces Foundation was established in 1987, providing educational programming and bursaries for post-secondary education. Since his death in 2012, the work of his foundation has been carried on by his daughter, Bernice Carnegie.

Making History

In the 2000–01 season, there were only 16 Black players in the NHL. Five of them — Mike Grier, Georges Laraque, Anson Carter, Joaquin Gage and Sean Brown — played for Edmonton. That season's high point was a nine-game winning streak in February, which got them to the playoffs. Twenty years later, they got together to talk about their NHL careers for Black History Month.

Laraque and Carter have both gone into media. Laraque hosts a radio show in Montreal. Carter has been a hockey analyst with several different U.S. networks and started a record label. Grier was the first Black player from the United States to make it to the NHL. He played 1,060 games over 14 seasons between 1996 and 2011 with Edmonton, Washington, Buffalo and San Jose. Then Grier became a scout, then an assistant coach, and then a hockey operations adviser with the Blackhawks, the Devils and the Rangers. On July 5, 2022, Grier returned to the San Jose Sharks when he was hired as the first Black general manager in NHL history.

Lost Leagues

Black people have a long history in Nova Scotia and formed thriving communities dating back to to the 1780s.

The Colored Hockey League of the Maritimes was formed in 1895. Among the main organizers were leaders of local Baptist churches who thought a hockey game between rival churches after services would boost attendance. The league originally had just three teams, but between 1900 and 1905, there were hundreds of players and more than 12 teams. Some of the teams during those first ten years were the Halifax Stanleys, the Halifax Eurekas, the Dartmouth Jubilees, the Africville Sea-Sides, the Truro Victorias, the Charlottetown West End Rangers, the Amherst Royals and the Hammond Plains Moss Backs.

It wasn't always easy for the Black teams to get ice time. Rink owners sometimes refused to rent to them, and even when they did, the teams had to wait until the white teams were finished playing. Games often had to be played outdoors, on local ponds. The last recorded newspaper accounts of the games in the original CHL appeared in 1911, but the league was reformed in 1921 with three teams: the Truro Victorias, the Africville Sea-Sides and the Halifax All-Stars. All the original organizers were deceased by this time, and after 1925, teams came and went very quickly. Black teams such as the Halifax Diamonds, the Halifax Wizards, the New Glasgow Speed Boys, the Africville Brown Bombers and the Truro Sheiks would compete at various points into the 1930s, but the league would soon be all but forgotten.

Fortunately, the CHL has returned to the public eye in recent years, with a book and documentary film called Black Ice.

In 2020, Canada Post issued a stamp featuring the 1906 CHL champion Halifax Eurekas.

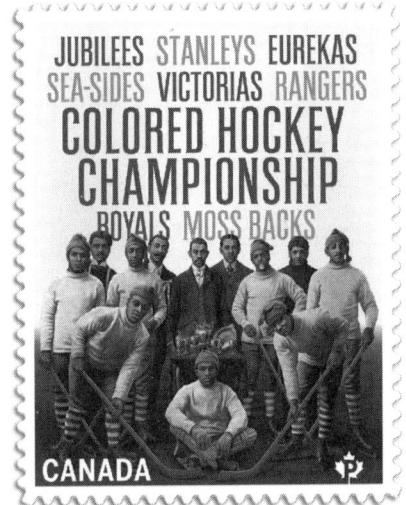

Dropping Down in History

There was no official rule book for games in the Colored Hockey League. As a result, games were often more physical than in white leagues. They were sometimes more innovative too. For example, the rules used in most hockey leagues used to forbid goalies from dropping down to the ice to make a save. A goalie could be given a penalty if he sprawled on the ice to stop the puck. The Pacific Coast Hockey Association changed the rule for the 1916–17 season, and the NHL followed suit at the start of its first season in 1917–18. Goalies quickly added the drop-down to their play.

But the one who did it first is goalie Henry "Little Braces" Franklyn of the Dartmouth Jubilees in the CHL. He was said to be dropping down to make saves as early as 1898.

A Shot that Slaps

Who invented the slapshot? It's hard to say. The slapshot is often credited to Bernie Geoffrion of the Montreal Canadiens in the 1950s. "Boom Boom" — as he was known — certainly helped popularize the slapshot, but he wasn't the first to use it. Bun Cook, who had started with the Rangers in 1926, might have been the one to introduce the slapshot to the NHL, but there are references in newspaper articles of players in the Colored Hockey League using it before that.

Eddie Martin played in the CHL with the Halifax Eurekas and the Africville Sea-Sides between 1899 and 1902. He was said to have had a very hard and accurate shot, and in the book *Black Ice*, authors George and Darril Fosty write that descriptions of his shooting style show that Martin may indeed have been the pioneer of the slapshot.

BY THE NUMBERS

The 2022–23 Boston Bruins set a new NHL regular-season record for wins and points. Here's a look at the top 10 regular-season win leaders in NHL history:

TEAM	SEASON	GP	W	L	T	OTL	POINTS
Boston Bruins	2022–23	82	65	12	0	5	135
Detroit Red Wings	1995–96	82	62	13	7	0	131
Tampa Bay Lightning	2018–19	82	62	16	0	4	128
Montreal Canadiens	1976–77	80	60	8	12	0	132
Montreal Canadiens	1977–78	80	59	10	11	0	129
Montreal Canadiens	1975–76	80	58	11	11	0	127
Detroit Red Wings	2005–06	82	58	16	0	8	124
Florida Panthers	2021–22	82	58	18	0	6	122
Boston Bruins	1970–71	78	57	14	7	0	121
Edmonton Oilers	1983–84	80	57	18	5	0	119

Count 'Em Up

The NHL currently has 32 teams, but how many teams have there been in the entire history of the NHL since 1917? Some teams have had a few different names over the years, like the Toronto Arenas, Toronto St. Patricks and the Toronto Maple Leafs. Other teams have moved from one city to another but are really still the same franchise. And two different teams have been known as the Ottawa Senators and the Winnipeg Jets. But if you count them all up, including city and name changes, the total comes to 60 NHL teams.

DID YOU KNOW?

When Boston beat the Edmonton Oilers 3–2 on February 27, 2023, they became the first team in NHL history to beat 31 other teams in the same season. Of course, there have been only 32 teams in the NHL since the 2021–22 season, but beating all 31 other teams in one season is pretty darned impressive!

Total Teams, Take Two

The very first NHL season started with four teams and soon dropped to three. It would take nine years to hit the ten-team mark, which happened for the 1926–27 season. But five years later, it fell to eight, and by 1942, dropped to six — the famous "Original Six." It stayed that way for 25 years! But in 1967 the NHL doubled, adding six new teams, which was the biggest expansion in professional sports history! Over the next 12 years, a couple of teams were added every few seasons. The NHL hit a total of 21 after adding four former World Hockey Association teams for the 1979–80 season. Expansion stopped again until 1991. New teams were added again at a slow, steady pace until hitting 30 teams in 2000. The NHL then took a 17-year pause until the 2017–18 season, when they added the Vegas Golden Knights. Most recently, the Seattle Kraken was added in 2021, bringing the total NHL teams to 32.

Post-Play Progress

In recent years, an increasing number of women have been hired to high-profile jobs with NHL teams. Hayley Wickenheiser and Danielle Goyette, who starred together for years with the Canadian national women's team, both work for the Toronto Maple Leafs. Wickenheiser is an assistant general manager, while Goyette is the director of player development. Former U.S. Women's National Team star Cammi Granato is one of two women who are assistant general managers for the Vancouver Canucks. Current Canadian women's star Marie-Philip Poulin is a player development consultant with the Montreal Canadiens.

There are more women than ever on coaching and scouting staffs too. One of these is Brigette Lacquette, who was brought on board by the Chicago Blackhawks in 2021. Lacquette is also the first Indigenous woman to scout for an NHL team.

Did You Know?

Before she became the first woman to play in the NHL in exhibition games with the Tampa Bay Lightning in 1992 and 1993, Manon Rhéaume was the first girl to play at the Quebec International Pee Wee Tournament in 1984. The first girls team to play at the tournament was the Équipe Québec Féminin, which began competing in 2016.

Fair Play

In 2023, the Quebec International Pee Wee Tournament added its first all-girls division. It was made up of 12 teams from Canada, the United States and Europe. The first champions of the girls division were the Durham West Lightning from the Pickering-Ajax area of southern Ontario (just east of Toronto). They beat the Atlantic Girls Selects 3–1 in the championship game.

Trophy Tales

The Quebec International Pee-Wee Tournament named a new award in 2023: the Guy Lafleur Trophy. It goes to the best player in the final of the AAA class, the highest category of the tournament. Before becoming an NHL legend, Lafleur had led his team to three straight championships at the tournament in 1962, 1963 and 1964, when he was 10, 11 and 12 years old.

DID YOU KNOW?

The Quebec International Pee-Wee Tournament was founded in 1960, with 28 teams competing that year. Most were local, but a team from Boston, Massachusetts attended, and a team from Scarborough, Ontario won.

Goalies Rule

Rules 5.1 and 5.3 in the NHL Rulebook state:

> *A team shall be composed of 20 players (18 skaters and two goalkeepers)... Each team shall be allowed one goalkeeper on the ice at one time.*

Most NHL teams used to carry a single goalie on their roster. A new rule was introduced prior to the playoffs in 1965 requiring each team to dress two goalies for playoff games. This change was added to the rule book for the regular season too, beginning with the 1965–66 season.

Double Trouble

In a January 2015 game, a team from Tefany High School in New Jersey knew they'd have it tough against rival team St. Joseph's. So Tefany decided to start their two goalies in net at the same time. But the referees wouldn't go for it. Right after the opening faceoff, Tefany was given a penalty for delay of game and had to remove the extra goalie. St. Joseph's went on to a 10–0 win.

Fifty years earlier, on December 23, 1964, a coach in a Rhode Island high school game tried something similar. His team, North Providence High, was facing a powerhouse opponent from Cranston East. So the North Providence coach put their starting goalie in the net and sent out their backup goalie dressed like a regular skater but wearing a goalie mask and gloves. The referees allowed it, but the high-scoring Cranston East team got the first goal just 55 seconds after the opening faceoff and led 5–1 after one period. That ended the two-goalie experiment. Cranston East went on to a 12–4 victory.

A Sticky Situation

Hall of Famer Martin Brodeur played 22 seasons in the NHL. He spent 21 years with the New Jersey Devils from 1992 to 2014, and played a final season with the St. Louis Blues in 2014–15. Brodeur set many regular-season records for goalies during his career, including most career wins (691) and most career shutouts (125). He also holds the record for most regular-season games played by a goalie, with 1,266 — and in each and every one of those games, Brodeur used a new stick. He explained his stick habit in his book *Martin Brodeur: Beyond the Crease*.

"I play with a new stick every game, so the first thing I do at the rink is get my sticks ready. I'll use one for warmup, one to play, and have three new ones on the bench. Some of the sticks I may use later for practice. I mark the ones I use in games on the knob with the date and the opponent, so if I give them away to friends, family, or charity, that information is on the stick. I give away more than a hundred sticks every season."

A Stinky Situation

If you play hockey, you probably know that "hockey smell" — the sort of dirty/sour blend of sweat, plastic, and wet leather. NHL teams have specialists to deal with it. Equipment managers wash everything regularly using industrial washers and dryers. Teams have special ozone treatment machines to help gear stay fresh and odour-free.

For those without ozone machines, the best advice is to air out equipment every time. Most gear can be washed — except for helmets and skates — and put in the dryer — except leather gloves. Interior pieces of helmets and skates need to be removed and aired out. A wipe of hard plastic surfaces with disinfectant will also help tame that stinky hockey smell.

Read MORE hockey!

978-1-4431-9387-0

978-1-4431-4680-7

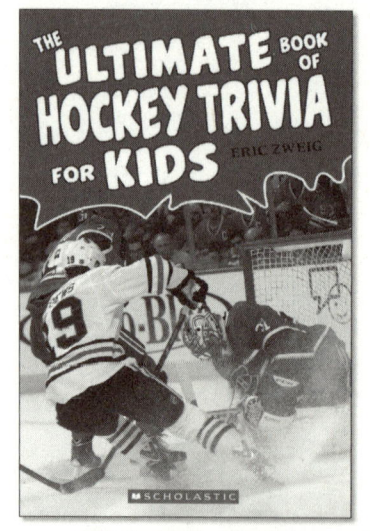

978-1-4431-4609-8

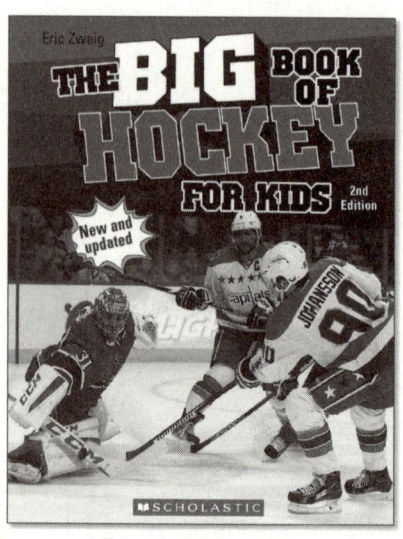

978-1-4431-4867-2